LEON

Breakfast & Brunch

NATURALLY FAST RECIPES

LEON

Breakfast & Brunch

NATURALLY FAST RECIPES

By Henry Dimbleby, Kay Plunkett-Hogge, Claire Ptak & John Vincent

PHOTOGRAPHY BY GEORGIA GLYNN SMITH · DESIGN BY ANITA MANGAN

conran
OCTOPUS

Contents

Introduction

Hubris is said to cause the collapse of empires. There's danger in getting too big for one's boots. In feeling invincible. More important than others. So, it is with some hesitancy that we confirm the rumor that breakfast probably is the MOST IMPORTANT MEAL OF THE DAY. It deserves a medal. Or at least a sash. Or a badge it can sew onto its tracksuit.

And it's true. Our own lives, serving people who eat with us at Leon, our research, and our work in school food, have all taught us the power of a good breakfast. It's why we've created the Leon Power Smoothie. It's why we focus so much effort on our oatmeal—try oatmeal and add a banana or dark chocolate topper (see page 10), and why we created the Posh Poached Eggs in a Cup made with chorizo and truffled cheese (see page 26). And it's why we've created a range of breakfast muffins made with spelt, a good alternative to modern wheat. And it's why we bring you this little book.

Now, let's keep things positive. Let's not preach that "commercial" cereals are mostly wheat and sugar, spiking blood sugar in a not-so-wonderful way. Let's instead explore and enjoy all of the ways we can release ourselves from the tyranny of that rectangular box.

We know you have a lot going on, so we've kept these recipes simple. But you can't make things using ingredients you don't have in your house. (Is that a bit obvious?) So a little thinking ahead will help with your mission.

Please share with us what ideas and approaches work well for you. For example, we find it good to combine good fats with good carbs; we have walnuts or seeds with our oatmeal. And when making pancakes, we make them with buckwheat, which is naturally free from gluten.

Most of all, we hope you find these recipes a wonderful way of enjoying your breakfasts, your morning, and your life. We like them.

Henry & John

GRAINS OF GOODNESS

Oatmeal

SERVES 2 • PREPARATION TIME: NONE • COOKING TIME: 5 MINUTES • ♥ ✓ WF GF DF V

Oatmeal, aka porridge, is enjoying something of a comeback after years in the highland wilderness. Not only is it low GI, which means it keeps you feeling full for longer, it also magically lowers cholesterol levels. And best of all, it's a perfect vehicle for all kinds of scrumptious toppings. We serve bucketfuls of the stuff at Leon every day and are registered addicts.

Basic Oatmeal

To make oatmeal quickly, use rolled oats—not the steel-cut ones, which take ages to cook. In the restaurants we make it with whole organic milk. At home we often make it with water—it depends how creamy you are feeling.

(Oats are gluten free, but have often been milled in a mill that also processes wheat. Be sure to check if this is important to you.)

> 1 cup **rolled oats**
> 2 cups **water** (or **milk**, or a combination of the two)
> **salt**

1. Put the oats, water, and a good pinch of salt into a saucepan and cook over medium heat for 4–5 minutes, stirring as you go.

2. Serve.

Classic oatmeal toppers

- Cold milk with honey, a dollop of jam or preserves, some dark brown sugar, or light corn syrup.
- As above, but with heavy cream (Sundays only).
- Banana slices and honey (see opposite).
- Crispy bacon and maple syrup (a favorite with Daddy Bear—see opposite).
- Fruity feast—an extravaganza of fresh fruit, compote, toasted nuts and seeds, and honey (see opposite).

Leon originals— favorites from the restaurant

- Valrhona chocolate flakes
- Banana, orange blossom honey, and toasted seeds
- Blackberry or strawberry compote

OPPOSITE: OATMEAL TOPPED WITH CRISPY BACON AND MAPLE SYRUP; A FRUITY FEAST; BANANA SLICES AND HONEY

A picture book by
WILLIAM STOBBS
The Story of the
THREE
BEARS
THE STORY OF THE THREE BEARS

Claire's Healthy Granola

MAKES 3½ LBS (A GOOD AMOUNT) • PREPARATION TIME: 10 MINUTES
COOKING TIME: 1 HOUR 40 MINUTES • ♥ ✓ WF GF DF V

You will not believe how good this tastes. It is light and clustery.

10 cups **buckwheat flakes**
1 cup **whole almonds** (skins on)
½ cup **ground flaxseeds**
⅓ cup **sesame seeds**
¼ cup **pumpkin seeds**
¼ cup **amaranth**
1 cup **agave syrup**
¼ cup **olive oil** (not extra virgin)
½ cup **coconut oil**

½ cup **water**
1½ teaspoons **vanilla extract**
½ teaspoon **ground cinnamon**
a grating of **fresh nutmeg**
a pinch of **sea salt**
⅔ cup **golden raisins**
¾ cup **dry, unsweetened shredded coconut**

1. Heat the oven to 300°F. Line 2 baking sheets with parchment paper.

2. Put the buckwheat flakes, whole almonds, flaxseeds, sesame seeds, pumpkin seeds, and amaranth into a large bowl and set aside.

3. In a saucepan, combine the agave syrup, olive oil, coconut oil, and water. Place over medium heat and whisk constantly to melt it all together without burning.

4. Remove the syrup mixture from the heat and stir in the vanilla, spices, and salt. Pour the syrup onto the dry ingredients and stir well to completely coat all the nuts and seeds.

5. Spread the mixture out on the baking sheets and place in the oven for approximately 1 hour.

6. Remove from the oven, toss the mixture well with a metal spatula and return to the oven. Lower the temperature to 275°F and bake for another 35–40 minutes, or until the mixture is golden. Remove from the oven and allow to cool completely before stirring in the golden raisins and dry shredded coconut. Store in an airtight container.

TIPS

* Serve with fresh dates and low-fat plain yogurt for a naturally sweet treat.

Hazelnut Milk

MAKES ABOUT 2½ CUPS • PREPARATION TIME: 10 MINUTES + SOAKING TIME OVERNIGHT
COOKING TIME: NONE • ♥ ✓ WF GF DF V

¾ cup **hazelnuts,** soaked overnight or
    for 8 hours in chlorine-free water,
    drained, and rinsed
seeds from ¼ of a **vanilla bean**
2 tablespoons **raw honey**
    (preferably crystallized)
2½ cups **water**
a tiny pinch of **sea salt**

1. In a blender, blend the soaked hazelnuts, vanilla seeds, and honey with 1 cup of the water until almost smooth.

2. Add the remaining water and blend to mix.

3. Strain through a nut-milk bag, fine-mesh cheesecloth, or similar.

4. Chill and enjoy. Keeps for 6–8 days in the fridge.

Pumpkin Seed Milk

MAKES ABOUT 3¼ CUPS • PREPARATION TIME: 15 MINUTES + SOAKING TIME OVERNIGHT •
COOKING TIME: NONE • ♥ ✓ WF GF DF V

1½ cups **pumpkin seeds**, soaked overnight
   or for 6–8 hours in chlorine-free water,
   drained, and rinsed
⅓ cup **cashew nuts**, soaked overnight or for
   6–8 hours in chlorine-free
   water, drained, and rinsed
2 **dates,** pitted
1 tablespoon **maple syrup**
6 strokes of **grated nutmeg** (optional)
a pinch of **sea salt**
3 cups **water**

1. In a blender, blend all the ingredients with 1¾ cups of the water until almost smooth.

2. Add the remaining water and blend together.

3. Strain through a nut-milk bag, fine-mesh cheesecloth, or similar.

4. Chill and enjoy. Keeps for 6–8 days in the fridge.

TIPS

* To make this milk 100 percent raw, omit the cashew nuts, maple syrup, and ½ cup of water. Add 1 or 2 more dates.

Wonderful Yogurt

WF GF V

1. Fill a bowl with rich plain yogurt and cover liberally with rose petal jam (available from Middle Eastern grocery stores).

Swiss-style Muesli

MAKES 2 CUPS · PREPARATION TIME: 12 HOURS · COOKING TIME: NONE · ♥ ✓ WF GF V

1⅔ cups **rolled oats**
1⅔ cups **apple juice**

1. In a large bowl or plastic container with an airtight lid, mix the oats with the apple juice, cover, and refrigerate overnight.

TIPS

* Add flaxseeds or any other seeds you may desire. Soaking flaxseeds overnight helps release their Omega-3 oils.

* Fantastic eaten with plain yogurt and plenty of chopped fruit.

Mini Knickerbocker Glory

SERVES 2 • PREPARATION TIME: 5 MINUTES • COOKING TIME: NONE • ♥ ✓ V

1 small **mango**
1¼ cups **plain yogurt**
1–2 tablespoons **blackberry compote** or **preserves**

1 tablespoon **honey**
⅔ cup **granola**

1. Peel and chop the mango into little cubes.

2. Take 2 clean medium glasses and spoon a layer of yogurt into the bottom of each one.

3. Top this with compote, followed by honey, and a further layer of yogurt.

4. Scatter with chopped mango then top each serving with granola.

A Breakfasty Banana Split

SERVES 2 • PREPARATION TIME: 10 MINUTES • COOKING TIME: 5 MINUTES • WF GF V

2 **bananas**
1 **apple**
⅓ cup **nuts**—cashew nuts, hazelnuts, macadamias
1 tablespoon **butter**

2 tablespoons **plain yogurt**
1 tablespoon **honey**
2 tablespoons **Swiss-style muesli** (see page 16)

1. Peel the bananas and cut them in half lengthwise.

2. Core and coarsely chop the apple. Toast the nuts in a dry skillet over medium heat, then remove and coarsely chop.

3. Heat the butter in a heavy skillet, add the honey, and cook the bananas flat-side down for 3 minutes, or until golden.

4. In a clean bowl mix together the yogurt, the muesli, the chopped apple, and the toasted nuts.

5. Set the bananas on your breakfast plate (2 halves each), and top with the yogurt and nut mixture.

WEEKEND TREATS

Jonny Jeffrey's Fluffy Eggs

SERVES 4 • PREPARATION TIME: 10 MINUTES • COOKING TIME: 8–10 MINUTES • ✓ V

This is a fantastic Sunday breakfast recipe from Kay's friend Jonny Jeffery. It's one of those classic family recipes—something his grandmother used to cook for the kids as a treat.

4 **eggs**
4 slices of **bread**
small handful of finely shredded **cheese—Cheddar,**
   Parmesan, **Swiss**, whichever you prefer
salt and **freshly ground black pepper**

1. Heat the oven to 375°F.

2. Separate the eggs, keeping the yolks whole, and whisk the egg whites into stiff peaks.

3. Lightly toast the bread, then put the slices on a baking sheet. Spread three-quarters of the egg white onto the semitoasted bread.

4. Make a small well in the egg white on each slice of toast, and put an egg yolk into it, using one yolk per slice. Season each yolk with salt and pepper, then cover with the remaining egg white, making sure the yolk is sealed in.

5. Sprinkle a teaspoon of shredded cheese on top of each, then bake in the oven for 8–10 minutes, or until the top is nicely golden. This should give you a runny yolk. If you prefer a firmer yolk, give it a little longer in the oven. Serve at once.

When we were kids, we used to call our granny More Granny because we were always saying, "Please can we have some more, Granny?" Her fluffy eggs were always one of my favorites.

JONNY

TIPS

* When Jonny cooked this for us, he served it with some delicious pan-fried chorizo, but you could try serving it with bacon, smoked salmon, or even some sautéed mushrooms.

* Why not, as Jonny suggests, use duck eggs instead? Then you can call it Fluffy Ducks.

* The surface area of your slice of toast is important. The smaller the slice, the higher you must pile your egg whites, which slightly affects the cooking time. We recommend slices from a large white or brown loaf.

Perfect Scrambled Eggs

In the short story *007 in New York*, Ian Fleming gives one of the definitive recipes for scrambled eggs with cream and finely chopped *fines herbes*. But let's save the full Bond for the weekend. For an everyday breakfast, we won't be quite so indulgent.

5 **medium eggs**
a dash of **milk**
a good pinch of chopped **fresh parsley,**
   or **basil**, or **cilantro**, or **thyme** (optional)
1 tablespoon **butter**
salt and **freshly ground black pepper**

1. Crack the eggs into a bowl, add the milk, salt, and pepper (and the pinch of chopped herbs, if you're using them), and beat them all together with a fork.

2. In a heavy saucepan, melt the butter over medium heat until it starts to foam. Pour in the eggs, and start stirring at once with a fork or a wooden spoon. Keep stirring constantly as the eggs begin to come together.

3. The question now is: How runny do you like them? As the eggs begin to come together, start turning down the heat—they'll keep cooking in any residual heat. Keep stirring until you've got them just the way you like them, then serve out onto plates at once. Keep in mind, the eggs at the bottom of the pan will be firmer than the eggs you serve first—just in case some people prefer them one way or the other.

4. Garnish with an extra grind of black pepper and tuck in.

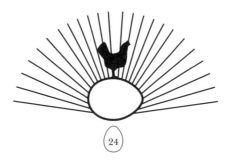

Perfect Poached Eggs

SERVES 4 • PREPARATION TIME: 10 MINUTES • COOKING TIME: 1.5 MINUTES • ✓ WF GF DF V

Kay never used to cook a lot of poached eggs until chef Bryn Williams, of Odette's in Primrose Hill, London, told her his infallible method. As he says, if you have to make fifty of the darned things a day, you want something foolproof. This is it.

4 **eggs**
1 teaspoon **salt**
1 tablespoon **white wine vinegar**
1 bowl of **iced water**—if you're
    not serving them immediately

1. Crack the eggs into 4 individual ramekins or small dishes.

2. Fill the deepest saucepan you can find with water, add the salt and vinegar, and bring to a rolling boil. One by one, add the eggs. They will sink to the bottom of the pan, and as they do, you will see the white coming up and around the yolk. After about a minute, the eggs will start to rise up through the water. At this point, if you're making them ahead of time, scoop the eggs out with a slotted spoon and plunge them immediately into the bowl of iced water to stop them from cooking. When they're cold, remove them from the water and set aside until you need them. If you're serving them now, cook them for a further 30 seconds to 1 minute in the boiling water for a firm white and a good runny yolk.

3. To reheat, bring a fresh saucepan of water to a boil, add the cooled eggs, and heat through for about 30 seconds to 1 minute.

TIPS

* **Perfect Soft-Boiled Eggs**
Ease an egg into salted boiling water and cook for 3 minutes and 33 seconds.

Posh Poached Eggs in a Cup

WITH CHORIZO & TRUFFLED CHEESE

SERVES 4 • PREPARATION TIME: 5 MINUTES • COOKING TIME: 10–15 MINUTES

On our breakfast menu at Leon, we have what we call Egg Cups. We poach eggs in a small pot and add a few things—the don't-you-ever-take-it-off-the-menu combination is truffle, Gruyère, and sliced chorizo. No chorizo on hand? It also works well with shredded ham or bacon. And once you've tried it, it'll never come off your breakfast menu either.

4–8 **eggs**
4 oz **chorizo**, thinly sliced
1 tablespoon **white vinegar**,
  for poaching
salt and **freshly ground**
  black pepper

For the cheese sauce:
2 tablespoons **unsalted butter**
¼ cup **chickpea flour**
1½ cups **milk**
1 cup **Gruyère cheese**, grated
½ teaspoon **truffle oil**

1. First make the sauce: melt the butter in a saucepan over medium heat. Add the chickpea flour and whisk the two together until smooth and all the flour is incorporated in the butter and cooks out—about 2 minutes.

2. Add the milk a little at a time, whisking as you go, until you have a smooth lump-free sauce. Keep whisking until it thickens slightly, enough to coat the back of a spoon. Add the shredded cheese and the truffle oil and whisk well until everything is combined and glossy, then season with salt and pepper. Set aside and keep warm.

3. In a nonstick saucepan, heat the olive oil over medium heat and fry the chorizo until the slices are cooked through and crisp. Remove the chorizo from the pan and drain on paper towels.

4. Poach the eggs (one or two each, depending on how hungry everyone is) following the method on page 25.

5. Grind some pepper and a little sea salt on top of each egg, then add them to their cups (I use a small teacup). Sprinkle one-quarter of the chorizo on top of each egg, then pour one-quarter of the cheese sauce over it and grind a little more pepper on top.

6. Nummy nummy, as John's daughter Natasha used to say.

Omelet Baveuse

THE WORLD'S GREATEST OMELET

PREPARATION TIME: 2 MINUTES • COOKING TIME: 2–3 MINUTES • ✓ WF GF V

Discovering an omelet "baveuse" is a game-changing moment in life. We were taught how to make them by our French friend Pierre. Many people leave the center of the omelet a little moist or tacky like this, but there is a particular quality that can only come from cooking them on low heat.

> 2 **eggs** per person
> 1 tablespoon grated **Cheddar cheese** per person
> 1 heaping spoonful of **crème fraîche** per person
> a dash of **vegetable oil**
> **sea salt** and **freshly ground black pepper**

1. Put the eggs, cheese, seasoning, and crème fraîche into a bowl. Whip them up a little with a fork so that they are well mixed.

2. Get a nonstick skillet reasonably hot and heat a dash of vegetable oil.

3. Pour in the egg mixture and tilt the skillet so it spreads around the bottom. With a rubber spatula, circle the edge of the pan and ensure that the edges remain loose. After 15 seconds reduce the heat to low.

4. When the top has a moist, tacky texture (see opposite), use the spatula to fold one side of the omelet over onto itself and slide it onto a plate. The omelet should be just colored on the underside, and still slightly runny inside.

5. Eat immediately.

TIPS

* If you want to make the omelet a little healthier you can leave out the cheese and crème fraîche (or replace the crème fraîche with a little whole milk).

* Thirty seconds into cooking you can add a filling. We particularly like:
  Healthy: Tomato and turmeric. Heat a little oil in a very hot skillet. Roughly chop a tomato (1 per person) and add it to the smoking oil. Toss vigorously—some of the oil may well flare up, so don't do this in flammable pajamas. Add a generous pinch of turmeric and season well. The tomatoes should still have shape but will be a bit saucy.
  Classic & Classy: Add fromage frais, smoked salmon, and chives.
  Cheesy: Add ½ cup more grated cheese per person, along with some chopped chives and parsley.
  Mushroomy: Put Ultimate Mushrooms on Toast (page 51) inside the omelet.
  Hammy: Prosciutto, crispy bacon, or any other finely diced cured meat.

French Toast

2 tablespoons **unsalted butter**, plus extra to serve
5 **eggs**
1¾ cups **whole milk**
1 tablespoon **pure vanilla extract**
⅓ cup **superfine sugar**
½ teaspoon **ground cinnamon**
8–12 slices of good **stale bread**
confectioners' sugar, for dusting
maple syrup, to serve

1. Heat a large heavy skillet over low heat and add a little of the butter.

2. In a large shallow bowl, whisk together the eggs, milk, vanilla, sugar, and cinnamon.

3. Place a couple of slices of bread in the eggy mixture and dunk it down, piercing the slices with tiny holes. Once the bread seems saturated, flip the slices over.

4. The skillet should now be ready and the butter sizzling.

5. Carefully lift the slices of bread from the eggy mixture and place in the skillet.

6. Brown the bread well on both sides, meanwhile repeating the dunking process with the next slice of bread.

7. Place on a plate, set in a warm place, and butter the slices.

8. Dust the finished slices of buttered French toast with confectioners' sugar and serve with maple syrup.

TIPS

* You can use all types of white crusty bread, as well as sourdough if you prefer.

* Be sure to soak the bread with lots of eggy mixture. And don't be shy with the butter in the pan. You want a moist, custardlike middle and a crisp exterior.

* Serve with fresh berries in the summer.

* Try slices of ripe bananas with a pinch of cinnamon.

* Add orange or lemon zest to the eggy mixture for a nice bright flavor.

Deconstructed Huevos Rancheros

WITH A FRESH ROMANO PEPPER & CHILE SALSA

SERVES 4 • PREPARATION TIME: 15 MINUTES • COOKING TIME: 10 MINUTES • ♥ ✓ WF GF DF V

This Mexican breakfast dish is usually made with a fried egg, served on fried corn tortillas with refried beans and a cooked tomato and onion salsa on the side. All we've done here is pulled back on the oil by poaching the eggs, plumped for a fresh salsa, and served some simple black beans and steamed corn tortillas on the side making it lighter.

For the Romano pepper & chile salsa:
1 **Romano pepper**, seeded
1 **green Serrano chile,** seeded
2 **tomatoes**, seeded
1 **shallot**
2–3 cloves of **garlic**
a few leaves of **fresh basil**
a squeeze of **lime juice**
a dash of **olive oil**
salt and **freshly ground**
   black pepper

1 x 15-oz can of **black beans**
1 teaspoon **dried oregano**
4–8 **corn tortillas**
4 **eggs**
salt and **freshly ground**
   black pepper

1. First make the salsa: dice the pepper, chile, tomatoes, shallot, and garlic, and mix them together in a bowl. Rip in the basil leaves, add the lime juice and olive oil, and season with salt and pepper. Stir together, taste for seasoning, then set aside.

2. Now empty the black beans into a saucepan—don't strain them, because you want their liquid. Gently heat them, adding the oregano and a pinch of salt and pepper. Set aside to keep warm.

3. Wrap the corn tortillas in a clean dish towel and steam over boiling water (preferably in a tiered steamer) for just a couple of minutes, or until they are piping hot. Set aside to keep warm.

4. Finally, poach the eggs (see page 25). To serve, place 1 or 2 warm corn tortillas on each plate and top with the eggs, beans, and salsa.

TIPS

Be sure to use pure corn tortillas. We've found that a lot of the commercial tortillas available have wheat in them. This is also delicious with some sliced avocado or guacamole on the side.

The Full Works with Easy Poached Eggs

SERVES 2 • PREPARATION TIME: NONE • COOKING TIME: 20 MINUTES • ✓DF

Like many good things in life, this is all about timing.

2 **tomatoes**
2 large or 4 small, flat **portobello mushrooms**
olive oil
2 **eggs**
4 slices of your favorite **bacon**

2 fat or 4 thin link or patty **pork sausages**
1 slice of **bread** per person (optional)
sea salt and **freshly ground black pepper**

1. Turn your broiler on fairly high. Tear off a sheet of aluminum foil and put it shiny side-down on a broiler pan. Cut your tomatoes in half and put them at one end in a row, followed by a neat row of whole mushrooms. Drizzle everything with a little olive oil and season well. Now add the sausages to the broiler pan and place it under the broiler on the highest shelf.

2. Set up 2 teacups and tear off a piece of plastic wrap for each one. Line the teacups with the plastic wrap and crack an egg into each. (If you are a confident egg poacher and have superfresh eggs, just poach them your normal way at the end.)

3. Add the bacon to the broiler pan and return it to the broiler. Fill a small saucepan two-thirds full with water, and put it on high heat to boil.

4. Bring up the edges of the plastic wrap to a tight twist, leaving a little airspace next to the egg.

5. Turn the sausages and bacon over and return the pan to the broiler for a further 5 minutes.

6. Meanwhile, gently drop your egg packages into the boiling water in the pan, turn the heat down to a simmer, and set your timer for 4 minutes for soft eggs or 5 for hard.

7. While the eggs are cooking, make your toast, if you are having it.

8. Assemble your breakfast on 2 plates. The eggs will be fine out of the water, in their plastic wrap, for a minute or two.

Saturday Pancakes

SERVES 4 • PREPARATION TIME: 15 MINUTES • COOKING TIME: 15 MINUTES • ♥ WF

For a luxurious—but wheat free—start to Saturday morning.

3 **eggs**
1 cup **buckwheat flour**
1 large teaspoon **honey**
a large pinch of **baking powder**
generous ½ cup **organic milk**
sea salt

1. Separate the eggs. Place the yolks in a large bowl and add the buckwheat flour.

2. Add the honey, baking powder, and a pinch of salt and mix thoroughly. Slowly add the milk to make a smooth batter. You can do all this the night before.

3. In a separate bowl, whisk the egg whites to firm peaks and fold gently into the yolk mixture.

4. Heat a nonstick skillet, gently drop in spoonfuls of the batter, and cook for 2–3 minutes on each side.

TIPS

You can devise all kinds of toppings for your pancakes, but here are three of our favorites:

- **Luxury:** Caramelized apple and cream. Foam a pat of butter in a skillet, toss in diced apples (1 apple per person), a sprinkling of cinnamon, and a little sugar and sauté until brown. Remove from the heat and stir in some heavy cream at the end.

- **Fruity:** Blueberries, sliced banana, and agave syrup.

- **John's Chocolate Pancakes:** John will eat chocolate with almost anything. This makes a surprisingly good breakfast. Banana, grated semisweet chocolate (70% cocoa solids), and agave syrup.

Mixed Fruit

WITH GREEK YOGURT & BROWN SUGAR

SERVES 4 • PREPARATION TIME: 10 MINUTES • COOKING TIME: NONE • WF GF V

A straightforward breakfast or brunch treat that can be made a few hours ahead.

1 large ripe **mango**
1 **kiwi**
⅔ cup **blueberries** or **blackberries**
⅔ cup **strawberrie**s
1 **passion frui**t
2 cups **Greek yogurt**
3–4 tablespoons firmly packed **dark brown sugar**

1. Peel and cube the mango and kiwi and place in a large mixing bowl.

2. Add the berries and the passion fruit seeds and mix well.

3. Chose an attractive serving bowl, or individual bowls if you want, and spoon in the fruit mixture.

4. Top generously with the Greek yogurt, so that it covers the mixture in a thick layer.

5. Sprinkle with the dark brown sugar—it will start to soak into the yogurt, but you will notice that some remains in clumps and forms delicious toffeelike lumps.

TIPS

* Add more sugar if you want your breakfast swimming in it.

* If you are making this in advance, you can either add the sugar just before serving, or add it earlier, let it soak into the yogurt, and add extra at the last minute.

* Use any combination of fruit. Berries and pitted stone fruits work the best.

BREADS
&
BAKES

Gluten-free Bread

MAKES I LOAF • PREPARATION TIME: 20 MINUTES + I HOUR RISING TIME
COOKING TIME: 55 MINUTES • ♥ WF GF V

The gluten in a loaf gives it that chewy interior and tender crumb. Take the gluten out and you get something a little denser of crumb and a bit more cakelike. In its own right, however, it is very satisfying.

> 4 cups **gluten-free whole-wheat bread flour**
> ½ teaspoon **sea salt**
> 2 x 14-oz envelopes **dry active yeast**
> 2 tablespoons **honey**
> 1⅓ cups **milk**
> 1 tablespoon **apple cider vinegar**
> 2 tablespoons **olive oil**
> 2 **eggs**
> **poppy seeds**, for sprinkling

1. Grease an 8-inch loaf pan.

2. Combine the flour, salt, and yeast and set aside.

3. Warm the honey and milk slightly and remove from the heat. Add the vinegar and oil and beat in the eggs.

4. Add the wet ingredients to the dry ingredients and bring together to form a dough. Then shape the dough into a log. Place it in your prepared pan, sprinkle with water, and then scatter with poppy seeds to cover. Put the dough in a warm place and leave to rise for 1 hour.

5. Just before the dough finishes rising, preheat the oven to 400°F. When the dough has risen, add it to the oven and bake for 45–55 minutes.

6. Leave to cool in the pan for 5 minutes before turning out onto a wire rack to cool completely.

TIPS

* Try adding some seeds to the dough to vary the texture and flavor of this loaf. It is always a good idea to soak the seeds overnight before adding them to the bread mixture, because soaking the seeds increases the amount of vitamins your body can absorb from them.

Raw Nut & Seed Butters

One of the best things to spread on your bread first thing in the morning is a homemade nut butter. They are both indulgent and fantastically good for you.

1. Choose good-quality, very fresh raw walnuts, almonds, pumpkin seeds, hazelnuts, cashew nuts, or sunflower seeds.

2. If you like, you can soak or sprout the nuts or seeds first. If you do this, make sure you dry them well before processing them.

3. Process the nuts or seeds in a food processor for several minutes to extract all the oil. As the nuts and seeds are being processed, you can drizzle in a little raw honey or water to help turn it into an emulsified butter.

4. Store in the refridgerator.

Flour Station Rye Bread

MAKES I LOAF • PREPARATION TIME: I HOUR + I HOUR RESTING AND PROVING TIME
COOKING TIME: 55 MINUTES • ♥ ✓ WF D F V

We use this bread at Leon to make New York-style open sandwiches. It is baked for us by the magnificent bakers at London's Flour Station, who add baked potatoes to the dough to keep it moist, with nutty sunflower seeds giving some bite.

2 tablespoons **rye starter**
(50% water/50% rye flour)
1 medium **baking potato**
1½ teaspoons **water**
1 cup **rye flour**, plus extra
for dusting

½ oz **active dry yeast**
2 teaspoons **salt**
⅔ cup s**unflower seeds**
2 tablespoons **molasses**

1. First make your rye starter by stirring ½ cup rye flour and ½ cup of warm water together in a jar with a secure lid—a preserving jar is ideal. Seal with the lid and leave the jar in a prominent and warm place in your kitchen. Each day for a week repeat the feeding process by placing ½ cup of the starter in a bowl (discarding the surplus or using it to flavor cakes, buns, pancakes, or pizza dough), and adding ½ cup of warm water and ½ cup of flour. Stir vigorously with a clean finger or a fork to remove any floury lumps. Return it to the jar. After about 5 days you'll notice bubbles in the dough. This means it's ready to be used. From now on, you can keep it in the fridge, removing it a couple of days before use to feed it back into full bubbly liveliness.

2. Heat the oven to 425°F. Bake the potato, let it cool, and then peel it.

3. Put all the ingredients into a mixing bowl (avoiding direct contact between the fresh yeast and the salt).

4. In a stand mixer with a dough hook, mix on a slow speed until everything is blended, or mix by hand. The dough will be very wet and sticky, but after a while the color will change slightly from brown to a lighter, more yellow color.

5. Cover the bowl with a damp cloth and leave the dough to rest for approximately 3 hours, or until the dough is "active" or bubbling.

6. Butter a 9-inch loaf pan and dust it with rye flour.

7. Dust the work surface with rye flour and turn out the dough. Shape and place in the prepared loaf pan. Press down lightly and dust the top with rye flour.

8. Leave in a warm, draft-free place to "prove" (or rise), until you see cracks appearing on the surface of the dough. It should increase in size by approximately 50 percent.

9. When the dough has nearly finished proving, heat the oven to 425°F again. Dust the dough with rye flour once more and bake in the oven for 55 minutes, or until the loaf has a richly colored, dark crust.

TIPS

* This bread actually improves with age and is best enjoyed the day after baking. It will stay fresh for at least a week, because the potatoes attract moisture and therefore keep the bread moist for longer.

* Toast thin slices of this bread and top with butter or coconut oil and a Nut Butter (see page 45).

Topped Rye Bread

Of all the quick breakfasts, these are the quickest. Rye bread freezes well and toasts directly from frozen. It is wheat, and often yeast, free. Most importantly, the modern rye breads no longer taste of Ukrainian footwear. They are soft and sweet and remarkably addictive.

What follows are ideas rather than recipes—we hope they will spark you into making some rye creations of your own.

New York Breakfast WF

The classic rye breakfast. Toast the rye. Smear on cream cheese. Top with smoked salmon, cucumber rings, diced ripe tomatoes, and finely sliced red onion. Squeeze some lemon juice on top and scatter with chopped chives.

Cream Cheese & Blueberry Preserves WF V

Think yogurt and preserves, but on an open sandwich.

Peanut Butter & White Grapes ♥ WF DF V

This is the healthy version of peanut butter and jelly. Slice the white table grapes in half and either place them loosely on the peanut butter or arrange them in military rows for that classic 70s look.

Other rye toppers we love

- **The European:** Like the New York breakfast, but substitute a good ham for the smoked salmon.

- **The Fruit & Nut:** Any other combination of fruit and peanut butter. Finely sliced apple is particularly good.

- **Hot Berries:** In a saucepan, warm honey, ground cinnamon, and berries until the berries begin to lose their edges. Dollop onto the rye and top with a spoonful of yogurt.

- **The Wimbledon:** Strawberries and banana tossed in a little thick yogurt, with a touch of honey drizzled on top.

- **Honey & Banana Slices:** Spread the honey on the rye and arrange the banana slices geometrically, just because it looks pretty.

- **The Full English:** Sliced tomatoes topped with scrambled eggs, and a slice of crispy bacon.

- **The Veggie English:** Sliced tomatoes, topped with mushrooms that have been quick-fried in superhot olive oil.

- **The Reichstag:** Wholegrain mustard spread on the rye covered with sliced tomatoes, ham, and finely sliced dill pickles. For extremists only.

Ultimate Mushrooms on Toast

A chef friend of ours once said he believed that the common white mushroom would be an expensive delicacy if it were rare. The way it changes color and deepens in flavor as it cooks is a wonder, so don't feel you need fancy mushrooms to make the ultimate mushrooms on toast.

1. A slice of good bread, toasted.

2. Butter, spread on the toast.

3. A good pat of butter and a trickle of vegetable oil in a hot saucepan. The butter should foam.

4. A generous handful of sliced button mushrooms thrown into the pan with a tablespoon of finely sliced onion. Don't move them around too much. Toss every 30 seconds or so, but give them time to turn golden. Season with salt and pepper.

5. Minced garlic and chopped fresh parsley thrown in for the last 30 seconds.

6. Add a squeeze of lemon juice then spoon the mixture onto the toast.

Variations on a theme

- **Luxury:** Instead of lemon juice, add a splash of white wine at the end. When this has bubbled off, add a tablespoon of heavy cream and let it bubble for 20 seconds before transferring the mixture to the toast.

- **Meaty:** Before you cook the mushrooms, fry some prosciutto in the pan until it gets crispy. Stick it on top like a shark's fin.

- **Toast on Mushrooms on Toast:** This was an accident we discovered while photographing the pictures for this book. Nothing in the world tastes better. Fry some breadcrumbs with garlic and seasoning until they are crisp. Make the Ultimate Mushrooms on Toast then scatter with the garlic breadcrumbs for extra crunch to serve.

DRINKS

Ralph's Mango Lassi

SERVES 2 • PREPARATION TIME: 15–20 MINUTES • COOKING TIME: NONE • ♥ WF GF V

A wonderful, cooling drink, especially in hot weather, this is also a great fruity way to start the day.

1¼ cups **active yogurt** (low-fat if preferred), chilled
4 ripe chilled **mangoes**, peeled, pitted, and chopped
2 tablespoons **honey**
1 tablespoon **lime juice**
2 cups of **ice cubes**
sprigs of **fresh mint**, to garnish

1. Combine the yogurt, mangoes, honey, and lime juice in a blender. Add ice and blend for 15 seconds, until smooth.

2. Serve garnished with sprigs of mint.

TIPS

* You can use buttermilk in place of the yogurt, if you prefer.

* If you can't find decent ripe mangoes, you can buy unsweetened mango pulp in cans at most large supermarkets.

* For a less sweet version, omit the honey and add a teaspoon of salt and a couple of pinches of ground cardamom.

RALPH, BANGKOK, 1988

Lovely Ralph Monthienvichienchai is literally MADD about mangoes, so much so that he opened a dessert bar of the same name in London. If you need to know anything about mangoes, he's your guy. Thanks to him for this delicious recipe.

Hattie's Super-Healthy Almond Smoothie

SERVES 2 • PREPARATION TIME: 5 MINUTES • COOKING TIME: NONE • ♥ WF DF GF V

And for those who are looking for something dairy free…

1 **kiwi**
1 **banana**
2 large handfuls of **berries**—whatever is in season
8 **almonds**, skins on
2 heaping tablespoons **rolled oats**
1 tablespoon **pumpkin seeds**
1 tablespoon **sunflower seeds**
1 cup **rice milk**, **almond milk**, or **soy milk**

1. Peel the kiwis and the banana. Wash the berries.

2. Put all the ingredients into a smoothie machine or a blender and blend together until smooth.

Tiger's Milk

SERVES 1 • PREPARATION TIME: 3 MINUTES • COOKING TIME: 2–3 MINUTES • WF GF V

Tiger, Tiger, burning bright … No, no—not THAT kind of tiger! You think we're crazy enough to try to milk one? No, this was the only way anyone could get the small Kay to drink milk. The tale went that it was "tiger's milk" because it was striped. Kay can't for the life of her believe that she fell for that one! The honey "stripes" disappear after about three seconds, so she must have been an extraordinarily gullible child!

1 mug of **milk**
1 small **stick of cinnamon**
1 tablespoon **honey**
an extra pinch of **ground cinnamon** (optional)

1. Heat the milk in a saucepan until it's just warm—you don't want it too hot. Then use an immersion blender to froth the milk. This guarantees you will get stripes.

2. Pop the cinnamon stick into the mug and pour the warmed milk over it. Now—watch for it—drizzle the spoonful of honey into the milk, from a height, in concentric circles. See those stripes? Stir it in with the cinnamon stick and add an extra pinch of cinnamon, if you like.

LUNE & KAY, 1965

Lune was a huge part of our family, and was my nanny when I was growing up. She was also the manufacturer of this particular tall tale. We adored each other. Except for when she tried to comb the tangles out of my perpetually wayward hair. Then I wasn't so fond of her.

KAY

CONVERSION CHART FOR COMMON MEASURES

LIQUIDS

15 ml	$^1/_2$ fl oz
25 ml	1 fl oz
50 ml	2 fl oz
75 ml	3 fl oz
100ml	3 $^1/_2$ fl oz
125 ml	4 fl oz
150 ml	$^1/_4$ pint
175 ml	6 fl oz
200 ml	7 fl oz
250 ml	8 fl oz
275 ml	9 fl oz
300 ml	$^1/_2$ pint
325 ml	11 fl oz
350 ml	12 fl oz
375 ml	13 fl oz
400 ml	14 fl oz
450 ml	$^3/_4$ pint
475 ml	16 fl oz
500 ml	17 fl oz
575 ml	18 fl oz
600 ml	1 pint
750 ml	1 $^1/_4$ pints
900 ml	1 $^1/_2$ pints
1 liter	1 $^3/_4$ pints
1.2 liters	2 pints
1.5 liters	2 $^1/_2$ pints
1.8 liters	3 pints
2 liters	3 $^1/_2$ pints
2.5 liters	4 pints
3.6 liters	6 pints

WEIGHTS

5 g	$^1/_4$ oz
15 g	$^1/_2$ oz
20 g	$^3/_4$ oz
25 g	1 oz
50 g	2 oz
75 g	3 oz
125 g	4 oz
150 g	5 oz
175 g	6 oz
200 g	7 oz
250 g	8 oz
275 g	9 oz
300 g	10 oz
325 g	11 oz
375 g	12 oz
400 g	13 oz
425 g	14 oz
475 g	15 oz
500 g	1 lb
625 g	1 $^1/_4$ lb
750 g	1 $^1/_2$ lb
875 g	1 $^3/_4$ lb
1 kg	2 lb
1.25 kg	2 $^1/_2$ lb
1.5 kg	3 lb
1.75 kg	3 $^1/_2$ lb
2 kg	4 lb

OVEN TEMPERATURES

225°F ......(110°C) ......Gas Mark $1/4$
250°F ......(120°C) ......Gas Mark $1/2$
275°F ......(140°C) ......Gas Mark 1
300°F ......(150°C) ......Gas Mark 2
325°F ......(160°C) ......Gas Mark 3
350°F ......(180°C) ......Gas Mark 4
375°F ......(190°C) ......Gas Mark 5
400°F ......(200°C) ......Gas Mark 6
425°F ......(220°C) ......Gas Mark 7
450°F ......(230°C) ......Gas Mark 8

MEASUREMENTS

5 mm .... $1/4$ inch
1 cm .... $1/2$ inch
1.5 cm .... $3/4$ inch
2.5 cm .... 1 inch
5 cm .... 2 inches
7 cm .... 3 inches
10 cm .... 4 inches
12 cm .... 5 inches
15 cm .... 6 inches
18 cm .... 7 inches
20 cm .... 8 inches
23 cm .... 9 inches
25 cm .... 10 inches
28 cm .... 11 inches
30 cm .... 12 inches
33 cm .... 13 inches

Working with different types of oven

All the recipes in this book have been tested in an oven without a fan. If you are using a convection (fan-assisted) oven, lower the temperature setting by 25°F. Convection ovens circulate heat evenly and efficiently around the oven, so there's no need to worry about where to position the baking dish.

Regardless of what type of oven you use you will find each has its idiosyncrasies, so don't stick slavishly to any baking recipe instructions. Make sure you understand how your oven behaves and adjust to that.

Key to Symbols/Nutritional Info

♥   LOW SATURATED FATS
✓   LOW GLYCEMIC (GI) LOAD
WF   WHEAT FREE
GF   GLUTEN FREE
DF   DAIRY FREE
V   VEGETARIAN
Ⓦ   INDULGENCE

🐦   COOKING TIPS, EXTRA INFORMATION,
TIPS   AND ALTERNATIVE IDEAS.

Index

First published in Great Britain in 2013 by Conran Octopus Limited,
a part of Octopus Publishing Group,
Endeavour House, 189 Shaftesbury Avenue, London WC2H 8JY
www.octopusbooks.co.uk

An Hachette UK Company
www.hachette.co.uk

Distributed in the US by Hachette Book Group USA
237 Park Avenue, New York NY 10017 USA

Distributed in Canada by Canadian Manda Group
165 Dufferin Street, Toronto, Ontario, Canada M6K 3H6

Publisher: Alison Starling
Senior Editor: Sybella Stephens
Assistant Editor: Stephanie Milner
Art Director: Jonathan Christie
Art Direction, Design & Illustrations: Anita Mangan
Design Assistant: Abigail Read
Photography: Georgia Glynn Smith
Production Manager: Katherine Hockley

ISBN 978 1 84091 634 8

Printed in China

A note from the authors…
Medium eggs should be used unless otherwise stated.
We have endeavored to be as accurate as possible in all the preparation and cooking times listed
in the recipes in this book. However they are an estimate based on our own timings during recipe
testing, and should be taken as a guide only, not as the literal truth. We have also tried to source
all our food facts carefully. However, we are not scientists, so our food facts and nutrition advice
are not absolute. If you feel you require consultation with a nutritionist, consult your family doctor or
healthcare provider for a recommendation.